Shigeru Ban
Builds a Better World

Isadoro Saturno · Illustrated by Stefano Di Cristofaro

A note to the reader

When there are disasters in which people lose their homes, such as earthquakes, floods, or war, world-famous architect Shigeru Ban is frequently on the scene. He volunteers his time to design and help build emergency shelters. These structures are often constructed with inexpensive and recyclable paper tubing, a material that he is famous for using.

When Shigeru is not working to help disaster relief victims, he is busy designing major buildings like museums and office towers all over the world, from Tokyo to Paris to New York. And when he is not doing those things, he is teaching architecture students.

Shigeru Ban Builds a Better World is a book for children and families. Through the illustrated story, readers explore Shigeru's approach to designing buildings and his use of paper tubing. The separate booklet inside the book includes photographs of many of the emergency shelters Shigeru has designed. An interview with Shigeru and a timeline of his life provide valuable information about Shigeru and his work.

Tra Publishing's *Art For Good* series of books highlights artists, designers, and other creatives who, through their work, help people and the world. The series encourages readers to explore their own creativity and to think about ways they might also do good work.

"Even in disaster areas, as an architect

I want to create beautiful buildings.

I want to move people and to improve people's lives.

If I did not feel this way,

it would be impossible to create meaningful architecture

and to make a contribution to society

at the same time."

Shigeru Ban

In the world of things,
of objects,
there are those made of paper.

Lamps,

books...

"Chairs?"

Come, let's do an experiment.
Without any scissors or glue, let's create a small
paper house just by creasing and folding.

"I can draw a door for it!
And some windows,
and I can sketch our cat
waiting at the front door."

Can you imagine this house being as large as an actual house?
A house made entirely of paper and cardboard.

A house you could live in.

"No way! That would be impossible!"

Then you don't know **Shigeru Ban.**

I am from Japan,
and I always hold its buildings in my memory.

When I was a boy, I used to make wooden houses.

You need so little to be happy.

I don't like waste.

I want to protect the Earth
and, at the same time, to make beautiful things

for all human beings.

Shigeru is an architect who creates buildings
made of paper and cardboard.

"That doesn't make any sense."

Oh yes, it does.

Paper Arbor was the first building
that Shigeru made out of paper tubes.
He made it in Nagoya, Japan, in 1989.

This small pavilion withstood the worst
weather—rain and strong winds.

And there it stood for a long time.
Like a sculpture...made of paper.

"No way."

The paper tubes come in different sizes and are very sturdy.

They are so strong they can be used to build
a bridge that can hold the weight of twenty people,
and even some pets!

For Shigeru, these tubes are the bricks he has used to design all kinds of buildings: pavilions, theaters, houses, hotels…

"Look! I can see the stars

He has created many enormous and marvelous structures.

and planets!"

Shigeru quickly understood that his discovery
not only charmed the world with its beauty
but could also change people's lives.

"How?"

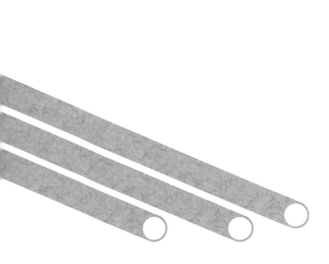

Shigeru Ban's Disaster Relief Projects

PAPER EMERGENCY SHELTER
Port-au-Prince, Haiti, 2010

Shigeru helped build emergency
shelters after a major earthquake hit
near Haiti's capital of Port-au-Prince,
causing extensive damage to buildings
and resulting in 1.2 million people
losing their homes.

Shigeru Ban's work in disaster relief started in 1994 when he saw news reports about the terrible living conditions of Rwandan refugees who fled a civil war in their country and were living in camps in Zaire (now the Democratic Republic of the Congo). He knew he wanted to help by creating better shelters.

Since then, **Shigeru** has traveled all over the world in order to help victims of disasters. He has created disaster relief buildings in places like Rwanda, Japan, China, India, Italy, Turkey, Sri Lanka, and Haiti. He also started the Voluntary Architects' Network in 1995 so that other people, especially students, can help build the shelters.

The shelters he designs are easy to build quickly, and they often use recycled paper tubes or other low-cost materials. In addition to temporary housing, **Shigeru's** emergency buildings include schools, churches, community centers, and even a concert hall.

These photographs are a selection of some of **Shigeru's** disaster relief projects.

PAPER LOG HOUSE
Bhuj, Gujarat State, India, 2001

The Gujarat Earthquake destroyed more than 300,000 buildings and damaged 700,000 more in the Bhuj-Ahmedabad-Rajkot region of India. Shigeru adapted his Paper Log House for India, with a shaded front area for people to spend time outdoors. The buildings' foundations were made from earthquake rubble covered with mud, and the roofs were made of bamboo. The photograph on the right shows the inside of one of the houses, which was used as a classroom.

PAPER LOG HOUSE
Cebu, Philippines, 2014

Typhoon Haiyan caused major damage, left many people homeless, and resulted in more than 6,000 deaths in the Philippines in 2013. Shigeru created a type of temporary shelter that combined his Paper Log House with his Paper Partition System. The foundations were Coca-Cola crates, the walls were bamboo mats, and the roofs were made from plastic sheeting and thatched palms. The walls let in light and air. These photographs show both the interior and exterior.

PAPER CHURCH
Kobe, Japan, 1995

The Great Hanshin-Awaji Earthquake in 1995 destroyed the Takatori Catholic Church. Shigeru offered to create a temporary church, but the priest said no. However, when he saw Shigeru's Paper Log Houses he changed his mind. The Paper Church was built in five weeks with help from 160 volunteers. Shigeru's building lasted in Kobe for ten years and then it was donated to replace a church destroyed in an earthquake in Taiwan.

CONTAINER TEMPORARY
HOUSING PROJECT
Onagawa, Miyagi, Japan, 2011

The Great Japan Earthquake and Tsunami
in 2011 destroyed or damaged almost
all of the 4,500 houses in Onagawa.
Shigeru designed multi-level temporary
housing from shipping containers.
He also created a community center using
containers and this atelier, or workspace.

PAPER PARTITION SYSTEM
Tohoku Region, Japan, 2011

As a result of the 2011 Great Japan Earthquake and Tsunami, 131,000 people had to leave their homes. Many were housed for months in group shelters in crowded conditions, such as this gymnasium. Shigeru set up his Paper Partition System in fifty shelters so that people could have some privacy.

CARDBOARD CATHEDRAL
Christchurch, New Zealand, 2013

A major earthquake in southern New Zealand in 2011 severely damaged the famous Christchurch Cathedral, built in the 1850s. Shigeru designed a temporary replacement cathedral using paper tubes. The building was large enough for 700 people. Shigeru also designed furniture out of wood and cardboard for the cathedral.

STUDENT VOLUNTEERS
Cebu, Philippines, 2014

Students from the University of San Carlos in Cebu helped build Shigeru's Paper Log Houses after Typhoon Haiyan, one of the strongest cyclones ever.

Shigeru creates structures to help people all over the world when they need places to live after losing their homes due to disasters, such as earthquakes, floods, or wars.

What is a permanent building and what is a temporary one?

A concrete building can be temporary if it's empty.

If no one wants it.

A paper building can be permanent as long as people love it.

A loved building will always remain.

"So my paper house...can last forever?"

The End

Let's learn more about **Shigeru Ban.**

Talking
With
Shigeru
Ban

Question: When you were young, you thought you would become a carpenter. That's partly because there were a lot of carpenters in your life! They were often working on your family's house, making it bigger because your mother's fashion business kept growing, and she needed more space. What was it about carpenters and carpentry that you liked?

Answer: *When my parents were having extensions added to our house, I liked to watch the carpenters. They used traditional Japanese methods, so they cut wood without using any machines. I thought they were magicians!*

Q: Why did you decide you wanted to be an architect?

A: *When I was a junior high school student, I learned how to design a house in a class in school, and I really found it joyful to learn. In addition, I was very happy that a model I created for a summer homework assignment was selected by teachers to be exhibited in the school.*

Q: You were a very good rugby player. You started playing when you were ten years old, and you were very involved in teams and in developing your skills for many years. What was it about rugby that you liked so much?

A: *The spirit of it. Rugby has a "One for all and all for one" spirit.*

Q: When you were very young, you played the violin. You started because your father loved music. And today, you love music. Did you like playing the violin?

A: *No, I didn't. Because I knew that I had no talent for music.*

Q: When it was time for you to go to college, you left Japan to study the United States. Why did you decide to do that?

A: *When I was a high school student, I picked up a magazine and read by chance about The Cooper Union and the works of the architect John Hejduk, who taught there. I became very interested in Hejduk and his work, and I decided to go there to study.*

Q: Going to The Cooper Union was a big deal! It meant going to another country, learning a whole new language, and it even meant going to another school first, the Southern California Institute of Architecture (SCI-Arc), because The Cooper Union did not accept international students directly. Was it hard to learn English?

A: *Yes! It was hard to learn English! And although I enrolled at SCI-Arc because I could not go directly to The Cooper Union, it became a very important part of my education as an architect.*

Q: After you graduated from college, it was not long before you opened your own architecture studio in Tokyo. What was the first building you designed?
A: *I built a building for my mother's atelier. It was my first work.*

Q: How interesting that all of the renovations on your childhood home—which were to make it larger for your mother's growing fashion business—led to your interest in houses and building. And then the very first building you designed was for your mother's business. What happened to that building?
A: *That building is now used as my office.*

Q: Did you design your house in Japan? What is it like?
A: *Yes. I live in an apartment building in Hanegi Forest in Tokyo. It was built without cutting down any of the trees in the forest. The trees grow in the round courtyards that are situated throughout the building.*

Q: Do you live in Japan year-round, or do you also live and work in other parts of the world?
A: *I live in Tokyo and go to Paris once every two weeks.*

Q: You often teach architecture students, and you have taught at universities all over the world. What is it about teaching that you like?
A: *I think teaching is one of the social responsibilities of an architect.*

Q: What advice do you have for people who would like to develop their creative skills, whether it is in architecture or painting or music or any other art form?
A: *Travel and see the whole world with your own eyes.*

Q: One of the major things you have pioneered is the use of paper tubes in your buildings—both your emergency shelters and also some of your other buildings, for clients. When did you first start using paper tubes?
A: *In 1986. The paper costs less than wood and can be used instead of wood.*

Q: You first used the tubes when you were designing an exhibition and could not afford wood. You had saved the paper tubes from inside rolls of paper in your office because you thought they might come in handy someday. And they did! After that you started experimenting a lot with them, and you soon started using them in buildings. Now you use them very often in your emergency shelters for disaster relief. Why are paper tubes a good material to use?
A: *Because paper is not a rare material, and it is easy to obtain in whatever country you are in.*

Q: You have designed so many types of buildings all over the world—houses, apartments, offices, stores, museums, libraries, huge towers, concert halls, sports stadiums, hotels, parks, train stations, schools, university departments, government buildings, and so much more. What would you like to do that you have not yet done?

A: *Someday I would like to build a winery.*

Q: What made you decide to help with disaster relief?

A: *Architects tend to work with the privileged classes of society. Historically speaking, it is people with money or political power who hire architects to express that power as something visible. The architecture then becomes a symbol of their status. I realized this when I started working as an architect, and it was actually very disappointing. But at the same time I also noticed how, when disasters happen, people lose their houses, or they suffer through lack of shelter, and I realized that this was where we could help.*

Q: And so you put your training as an architect to use in a way you never even knew existed when you first decided to become an architect. And your emergency shelters have now helped many thousands of people all over the world. Who builds the shelters that you design for victims of disaster?

A: *We work with local students and volunteers.*

Q: Your organization, Voluntary Architects' Network, involves many students who help when you go to disaster areas. Why do you feel it is important for students to be involved in this work?

A: *Well, they are free labor. I'm kidding, that's a joke! For me, it is very important to work with students. It is a good educational experience for them. They can learn a lot through these collaborations.*

Q: How do you think architects can do more good in the world?

A: *Each architect must be aware of his or her responsibility to society.*

Q: Do you have advice for people who want to help others, the way you do with disaster relief?

A: *First of all, you should know and find out in which area you could specialize.*

Q: What advice do you have for young people when it comes to choosing a career?

A: *Find and do what you love.*

Important Dates in Shigeru Ban's Life

1967
Learned to play the violin when he was young because his father loved classical music.

1963
Started school. He was very good at arts and crafts. He also loved to build things from pieces of wood. He wanted to become a carpenter.

1967
Started playing rugby. He loved it and went on to play on important teams.

1972
Decided he wanted to become an architect after making a model house for a school project.

1973
Beginning in 11th grade, he studied drawing every day after rugby practice.

1994
Became involved in helping disaster victims when he learned that Rwandan refugees were living in poor conditions.

1995
Used paper tubes for a disaster relief project for the first time. After the Kobe Earthquake in Japan, designed the Paper Log House for Vietnamese refugees and the Paper Church.

1993
Began teaching architecture at Tama Art University. Since then he has often taught.

1995
Created the Voluntary Architects' Network to work on disaster relief projects.

2000
His paper-tube architecture became known worldwide when he co-designed a huge structure for the Hanover Expo's Japan Pavilion.

2001
Time magazine named him the Innovator of the Year.

1960s
Favorite place to play with friends was in Hanegi Park, in a bomb shelter from World War II.

1957
Born in Tokyo, Japan. His father was a businessman who worked for Toyota, and his mother was a fashion designer. They lived in a wooden house.

1977–84
Attended college in the United States, at the Southern California Institute of Architecture (SCI-Arc) and then at The Cooper Union.

1978
Learned about the work of Buckminster Fuller and Frei Otto, both important influences.

1982–83
Worked at Arata Isozaki's firm.

1988
Married Masako, a jewelry and handbag designer.

1985
Started his own architecture firm in Tokyo. His first building was for his mother's fashion business. That building later became Shigeru's main office.

1984
Saw Alvar Aalto's architecture for the first time. Aalto was also an important influence.

2004
Won the competition to design the Centre Pompidou-Metz. He built an office made of paper tubes on a terrace at the Centre Pompidou in Paris.

2014
Awarded the Pritzker Architecture Prize, one of the most important awards in architecture.

Shigeru Ban has great advice for kids:

Find and do what you love.

Shigeru found what he loves: architecture.

He believes that architects have a responsibility to society.
He realized he could help people by providing emergency shelters
when there are disasters, and he works very hard to do that.

Now you've learned about how **Shigeru** thinks.

There are infinite ways to think, to be creative, and to help.

What would it mean to think like...you?

What might you do?

Many thanks to Shigeru Ban for his inspiring work, without which this book would not exist. And with gratitude to Shigeru Ban, Shigeru Ban Architects, and Yumiko Shirato for all of their help in the creation of this book.

Isadoro Saturno is an award-winning writer and editor with a specialty in children's books. His previous titles include *Conejo y Conejo* and *Samuel*. He started writing stories when he was six, beginning with a tale about a goat and its first trip to the ocean, which won third place in a writing contest.

Stefano Di Cristofaro is an award-winning illustrator and designer whose works have been widely exhibited. He has previously illustrated the children's books *And the People Stayed Home*, *Conejo y Conejo*, and *Guachipira va de viaje*. His family says that when he was little, he only stayed still if he was given a pencil and paper.

Author
Isadoro Saturno

Illustrator
Stefano Di Cristofaro

Publisher & Creative Director
Ilona Oppenheim

Art Director & Designer
Jefferson Quintana

Editor
Andrea Gollin

Editorial Contributor
Writer for introductory text,
insert booklet,
Shigeru Ban interview,
timeline
Andrea Gollin

Translator
Anna Kushner

Editorial Consultants
Ileana Oroza
Valentina Mendoza
Adam Dunlop-Farkas

Printing
Printed and bound in China
by Shenzhen Reliance Printers

Cover
Photograph: JOEL SAGET/AFP
via Getty Images
Cover design: Jefferson Quintana

First published 2023
by Tra Publishing
© 2023 Tra Publishing

Tra Publishing is committed to sustainability in its materials and practices. *Shigeru Ban Builds a Better World* is printed using soy-based ink. The book's primary text is printed on Forest Stewardship Council certified paper from well-managed forests. The paper used for the insert booklet, end pages, and cover is totally chlorine free and acid free and made from one hundred percent plant fiber that is recyclable and biodegradable.

ISBN: 979-8-9866406-3-1

Tra Publishing
245 NE 37th Street
Miami, FL 33137
trapublishing.com

 **tra.publishing**